D0283741

BY ADRIENNE RICH

A Wild
Patience Has
Taken Me
This Far

ADRIENNE RICH

A Wild Patience Has Taken Me This Far

POEMS 1978–1981

W · W · NORTON & COMPANY · NEW YORK · LONDON

Some of these poems were originally published in the following journals: *Conditions, Heresies, Iowa Review, Maenad, Massachusetts Review, Sinister Wisdom.*

Book design by Antonina Krass

Library of Congress Cataloging in Publication Data
Rich, Adrienne.
A wild patience has taken me this far: Poems 1978–1981.
Contents: The images—Coast to coast—
Integrity—[etc.]
I. Title.
PS3535.I233W48 1981   811'.54   81–4382
ISBN 0–393–01494–0   AACR2
ISBN 0–393–00072–9 (pbk.)

W. W. Norton & Company, Inc. 500 Fifth Avenue, New York, N.Y. 10110
W. W. Norton & Company Ltd. 25 New Street Square, London EC4A 3NT

3 4 5 6 7 8 9 0

CONTENTS

A Wild
Patience Has
Taken Me
This Far

THE IMAGES

Close to your body, in the
pain of the city
I turn. My hand half-sleeping reaches, finds
      some part of you, touch knows you before language
names in the brain. Out in the dark
a howl, police sirens, emergency
      our 3 a.m. familiar, ripping the sheath of sleep
   registering pure force as if all transpired—
the swell of cruelty and helplessness—
      in one block between West End
   and Riverside. In my dreams the Hudson
rules the night like a right-hand margin
      drawn against the updraft
   of burning life, the tongueless cries
of the city. I turn again, slip my arm
      under the pillow turned for relief,
   your breathing traces my shoulder. Two women sleeping
together have more than their sleep to defend.

And what can reconcile me
   that you, the woman whose hand
sensual and protective, brushes me in sleep,
      go down each morning into such a city?
   I will not, cannot withhold
your body or my own from its chosen danger
      but when did we ever choose _pornography + porn in the media_
   to see our bodies strung
in bondage and crucifixion across the exhausted air
      when did we choose
   to be lynched on the queasy electric signs
of midtown when did we choose
      to become the masturbator's fix

3

emblem of rape in Riverside Park   the campground
at Bandol   the beach at Sydney?
     We are trying to live
in a clearheaded tenderness—
I speak not merely of us, our lives
     are "moral and ordinary"
     as the lives of numberless women—
I pretend the Hudson is a right-hand margin
     drawn against fear and woman-loathing
The water is very
dangerous the surrounding (water as purification, river as boundary)
area is very dangerous but I know my imagination lies:
     in the name of freedom of speech *pornography is allowed*
     they are lynching us no law is on our side *to flourish*
there are no boundaries
     no-man's-land does not exist. *There is no place where*
          a patriarchal society doesn't exist.

I can never romanticize language again
     never deny its power for disguise for mystification
     but the same could be said for music
or any form created
     painted ceilings beaten gold worm-worn Pietàs
     reorganizing victimization   frescoes translating
violence into patterns so powerful and pure
     we continually fail to ask are they true for us.

When I walked among time-battered stones
     thinking already of you
     when I sat near the sea
among parched yet flowering weeds
     when I drew in my notebook
     the thorned purple-tongued flower, each petal
protected by its thorn-leaf
     I was mute
     innocent of grammar as the waves
irrhythmically washing   I felt washed clean
     of the guilt of words   there was no word to read

4

in the book of that earth   no perjury
the tower of Babel fallen once and for all   *reps. diff. languages - when the tower falls we have / languages*
    light drank at my body
    thinking of you I felt free
in the cicadas' pulse, their encircling praise.

    When I saw hér face, she of the several faces   *women of the past*
    staring   indrawn   in judgment   laughing for joy
her serpents twisting   her arms raised
        her breasts gazing
    when I looked into hér world
I wished to cry loose my soul
    into her, to become
        free of speech   at last.

And so I came home   a woman starving
        for images
    to say my hunger is so old
so fundamental, that all the lost
        crumbled   burnt   smashed   shattered   defaced
        overpainted   concealed and falsely named
faces of every past we have searched together
        in all the ages
    could rise   reassemble   re-collect   re-member
themselves as I recollected myself in that presence
        as every night close to your body
    in the pain of the city, turning
I am remembered by you, remember you
        even as we are dismembered
    on the cinema screens, the white expensive walls
of collectors, the newsrags blowing the streets
        —and it would not be enough.
This is the war of the images.
    We are the thorn-leaf guarding the purple-tongued flower
        each to each.

1976–1978

5

COAST TO COAST

There are days when housework seems the only
outlet   old funnel I've poured caldrons through
old servitude   In grief and fury bending
to the accustomed tasks   the vacuum cleaner plowing
realms of dust   the mirror scoured   grey webs
behind framed photographs   brushed away
the grey-seamed sky enormous in the west
snow gathering in corners   of the north

Seeing through the prism
you who gave it me
                    You, bearing ceaselessly
yourself   the witness
Rainbow dissolves the Hudson   This chary, stinting
skin of late winter   ice   forming and breaking up
The unprotected seeing it through
with their ordinary valor

Rainbow composed of ordinary light
February-flat
grey-white of a cheap enamelled pan
breaking into veridian, azure, violet
You write: *Three and a half weeks lost from writing*. . . .
I think of the word *protection*
who it is we try to protect   and why

Seeing through the prism   Your face, fog-hollowed   burning
cold of eucalyptus hung with butterflies
lavender of rockbloom
O and your anger uttered in silence word and stammer
shattering the fog   lances of sun
piercing the grey Pacific   unanswerable tide

6

carving itself in clefts and fissures of the rock
Beauty of your breasts   your hands
turning a stone a shell a weed a prism   in coastal light
traveller and witness
the passion of the speechless
driving your speech
protectless

If you can read and understand this poem
send something back: a burning strand of hair
a still-warm, still-liquid drop of blood
a shell
thickened from being battered year on year
send something back.

1978

INTEGRITY

the quality or state of being complete; unbroken condition; entirety
—Webster

A wild patience has taken me this far

as if I had to bring to shore
a boat with a spasmodic outboard motor
old sweaters, nets, spray-mottled books
tossed in the prow
some kind of sun burning my shoulder-blades.
Splashing the oarlocks. Burning through.
Your fore-arms can get scalded, licked with pain
in a sun blotted like unspoken anger
behind a casual mist.

The length of daylight
this far north, in this
forty-ninth year of my life
is critical.

The light is critical: of me, of this
long-dreamed, involuntary landing
on the arm of an inland sea.
The glitter of the shoal
depleting into shadow
I recognize: the stand of pines
violet-black really, green in the old postcard
but really I have nothing but myself
to go by; nothing
stands in the realm of pure necessity
except what my hands can hold.

Nothing but myself? . . . My selves.
After so long, this answer.

8

As if I had always known
I steer the boat in, simply.
The motor dying on the pebbles
cicadas taking up the hum
dropped in the silence.

Anger and tenderness: my selves.
And now I can believe they breathe in me
as angels, not polarities.
Anger and tenderness: the spider's genius
to spin and weave in the same action
from her own body, anywhere—
even from a broken web.

The cabin in the stand of pines
is still for sale. I know this. Know the print
of the last foot, the hand that slammed and locked that door,
then stopped to wreathe the rain-smashed clematis
back on the trellis
for no one's sake except its own.
I know the chart nailed to the wallboards
the icy kettle squatting on the burner.
The hands that hammered in those nails
emptied that kettle one last time   *I do domestic things as well*
are these two hands   *as things that men do.*
and they have caught the baby leaping
from between trembling legs
and they have worked the vacuum aspirator
and stroked the sweated temples
and steered the boat here through this hot
misblotted sunlight, critical light
imperceptibly scalding
the skin these hands will also salve.
                    Whatever danger there is I can tend to myself.
1978

9

CULTURE AND ANARCHY   *The bonds of female friendship +*
female support are at the heart of this poem.

Leafshade stirring on lichened bark
                              Daylilies
run wild, ''escaped'' the botanists call it
from dooryard to meadow to roadside

Life-tingle of angled light
                              late summer
sharpening toward fall, each year more sharply

This headlong, loved, escaping life

Rainy days at the kitchen table typing,
heaped up letters, a dry moth's
perfectly mosaiced wings, pamphlets on rape,
forced sterilization, snapshots in color
of an Alabama woman still quilting in her nineties,
The Life and Work of Susan B. Anthony. . . .

> *I stained and varnished*
> *the library bookcase today and superintended*
> *the plowing of the orchard. . . .*
> *Fitted out a fugitive slave for Canada*
> *with the help of Harriet Tubman. . . .*
> *The women's committee failed*
> *to report. I am mortified to death for them. . . .*
> *Washed every window in the house today.*
> *Put a quilted petticoat in the frame.*
> *Commenced Mrs. Browning's Portuguese*
> *Sonnets. Have just finished*
> *Casa Guidi Windows, a grand poem*
> *and so fitting to our struggle. . . .*
> *To forever blot out slavery is the only*

possible compensation for this
merciless war. . . .

The all-alone feeling will creep over me. . . .

Upstairs, long silence, then
again, the sudden torrent of your typing

Rough drafts we share, each reading
her own page over the other's shoulder
trying to see afresh

An energy I cannot even yet
take for granted: picking up a book
of the nineteenth century, reading there the name
of the woman whose book you found
in the old town Athenaeum
beginning to stitch together
Elizabeth Ellet
Elizabeth Barrett
Elizabeth Blackwell
Frances Kemble
Ida B. Wells-Barnett
Susan B. Anthony

On Saturday Mrs. Ford took us to Haworth,
the home of the Brontë sisters. . . .
A most sad day it was to me
as I looked into the little parlor where
the sisters walked up and down
with their arms around each other
and planned their novels. . . .
How much the world of literature has lost
because of their short and ill-environed lives

we can only guess. . . .

→

Anarchy of August: as if already
autumnal gases glowed in darkness underground
the meadows roughen, grow guttural
with goldenrod, milkweed's late-summer lilac,
cat-tails, the wild lily brazening,
dooryards overflowing in late, rough-headed
bloom: bushes of orange daisies, purple mallow,
the thistle blazing in her clump of knives,
and the great SUNFLOWER turns

Haze wiping out the hills. Mornings like milk,
the mind wading, treading water, the line of vision blind
the pages of the book cling to the hand
words hang in a suspension
the prism hanging in the windowframe
is blank
A stillness building all day long to thunder
as the weedpod swells and thickens
No one can call this calm

Jane Addams, marking time
in Europe: *During most
of that time I was absolutely at sea
so far as any moral purpose was concerned
clinging only to the desire to live
in a really living world
refusing to be content
with a shadowy intellectual
or aesthetic reflection*

finally the bursting of the sky
power, release

by sheets by ropes of water, wind
driving before or after
the book laid face-down on the table
spirit travelling the lines of storm
leaping the torrent   all that water
already smelling of earth

>Elizabeth Barrett to Anna Jameson:
>*. . . and is it possible you think*
>*a woman has no business with questions*
>*like the question of slavery?*
>*Then she had better use a pen no more.*
>*She had better subside into slavery*
>*and concubinage herself, I think, . . .*
>*and take no rank among thinkers and speakers.*

Early dark; still raining; the electricity
out. On the littered table
a transparent globe half-filled
with liquid light, the soaked wick quietly
drinking, turning to flame
that faintly stains the slim glass chimney:
ancient, fragile contrivance

light welling, searching the shadows

Matilda Joslyn Gage; Harriet Tubman;
Ida B. Wells-Barnett; Maria Mitchell;
Anna Howard Shaw; Sojourner Truth;
Elizabeth Cady Stanton; Harriet Hosmer;
Clara Barton; Harriet Beecher Stowe;
Ida Husted Harper; Ernestine Rose

and all those without names
because of their short and ill-environed lives

False dawn. Gossamer tents in wet grass: leaflets
dissolving within hours,
spun of necessity and
leaving no trace

The heavy volumes, calf, with titles in smooth
leather, red and black, gilt letters spelling:
THE HISTORY OF HUMAN SUFFERING

I brush my hand across my eyes
—this is a dream, I think—and read:
THE HISTORY OF WOMAN SUFFRAGE

> *of a movement*
> *for many years unnoticed*
> *or greatly misrepresented in the public press*
> *its records usually not considered*
> *of sufficient value to be*
> *officially preserved*

and conjure up again
THE HISTORY OF HUMAN SUFFERING
like bound back issues of a periodical
stretching for miles
OF HUMAN SUFFERING: borne,
tended, soothed, cauterized,
stanched, cleansed, absorbed, endured
by women

our records usually not considered
of sufficient value to be
officially preserved

> *The strongest reason*
> *for giving woman all the opportunities*

for higher education, for the full
development of her forces of mind and body. . .
the most enlarged freedom of thought and action
a complete emancipation
from all the crippling influences of fear—
is the solitude and personal
responsibility
of her own individual life.

➡

Late afternoon: long silence.
Your notes on yellow foolscap drift on the table
you go down to the garden to pick chard
while the strength is in the leaves
crimson stems veining upward into green
How you have given back to me
my dream of a common language
my solitude of self.
I slice the beetroots to the core,
each one contains a different landscape
of bloodlight filaments, distinct rose-purple
striations like the oldest
strata of a Southwestern canyon   *There is something left to*
an undiscovered planet laid open in the lens   *discover. This is optimistic.*

I should miss you more than any other
living being from this earth. . .
Yes, our work is one,
we are one in aim and sympathy
and we should be together. . . .

1978

FOR JULIA IN NEBRASKA

*Here on the divide between the Republican and the Little Blue lived some of
the most courageous people of the frontier. Their fortunes and their loves live
again in the writings of Willa Cather, daughter of the plains and interpreter of
man's growth in these fields and in the valleys beyond.*

*On this beautiful, ever-changing land, man fought to establish a home. In
her vision of the plow against the sun, symbol of the beauty and importance of
work, Willa Cather caught the eternal blending of earth and sky. . . .*

In the Midwest of Willa Cather
the railroad looks like a braid of hair
a grandmother's strong hands plaited
straight down a grand-daughter's back.
Out there last autumn the streets
dreamed copper-lustre, the fields
of winter wheat whispered long snows yet to fall
we were talking of matrices

and now it's spring again already.
This stormy Sunday lashed with rain
I call you in Nebraska
hear you're planting your garden
sanding and oiling a burl of wood
hear in your voice the intention to
survive the long war between mind and body
and we make a promise to talk
this year, about growing older

and I think: we're making a pledge.
Though not much in books of ritual
is useful between women
we still can make vows together
long distance, in electrical code:
Today you were promising me
to live, and I took your word,

Julia, as if it were my own:
we'll live to grow old and talk about it too.

I've listened to your words
seen you stand by the caldron's glare
rendering grammar by the heat
of your womanly wrath.
Brave linguist, bearing your double axe and shield
painfully honed and polished,
no word lies cool on your tongue
bent on restoring meaning to
our lesbian names, in quiet fury
weaving the chronicle so violently torn.

On this beautiful, ever-changing land
—the historical marker says—
man fought to establish a home
(fought whom? the marker is mute.)
They named this Catherland, for Willa Cather,
lesbian—the marker is mute,
the marker white men set on a soil
of broken treaties, Indian blood,
women wiped out in childbirths, massacres—
for Willa Cather, lesbian,
whose letters were burnt in shame.

Dear Julia, Willa knew at her death
that the very air was changing
that her Archbishop's skies
would hardly survive his life
she knew as well that history
is neither your script nor mine
it is the pictograph
from which the young must learn
like Tom Outland, from people

discredited or dead
that it needs a telling as plain
as the prairie, as the tale
of a young girl or an old woman
told by tongues that loved them

And Willa who could not tell
her own story as it was
left us her stern and delicate
respect for the lives she loved—
How are we going to do better?
for that's the question that lies
beyond our excavations,
the question I ask of you
and myself, when our maps diverge,
when we miss signals, fail—

And if I've written in passion,
Live, Julia! what was I writing
but my own pledge to myself
where the love of women is rooted?
And what was I invoking
but the matrices we weave
web upon web, delicate rafters
flung in audacity to the prairie skies
nets of telepathy contrived
to outlast the iron road
laid out in blood across the land they called virgin—
nets, strands, a braid of hair
a grandmother's strong hands plaited
straight down a grand-daughter's back.

1978, 1981

TRANSIT

When I meet the skier she is always
walking, skis and poles shouldered, toward the mountain
free-swinging in worn boots
over the path new-sifted with fresh snow
her greying dark hair almost hidden by
a cap of many colors
her fifty-year-old, strong, impatient body
dressed for cold and speed
her eyes level with mine

And when we pass each other I look into her face
wondering what we have in common
where our minds converge
for we do not pass each other, she passes me
as I halt beside the fence tangled in snow,
she passes me as I shall never pass her
in this life

Yet I remember us together
climbing Chocorua, summer nineteen-forty-five
details of vegetation beyond the timberline
lichens, wildflowers, birds,
amazement when the trail broke out onto the granite ledge
sloped over blue lakes, green pines, giddy air
like dreams of flying

When sisters separate they haunt each other
as she, who I might once have been, haunts me
or is it I who do the haunting
halting and watching on the path
how she appears again through lightly-blowing
crystals, how her strong knees carry her,

how unaware she is, how simple
this is for her, how without let or hindrance
she travels in her body
until the point of passing, where the skier
and the cripple must decide
to recognize each other?

1979

FOR MEMORY

Old words: *trust   fidelity*
Nothing new yet to take their place.

I rake leaves, clear the lawn, October grass
painfully green beneath the gold
and in this silent labor thoughts of you
start up
I hear your voice: *disloyalty   betrayal*
stinging the wires

I stuff the old leaves into sacks
and still they fall and still
I see my work undone

One shivering rainswept afternoon
and the whole job to be done over

I can't know what you know
unless you tell me
there are gashes in our understandings
of this world
We came together in a common
fury of direction
barely mentioning difference
(what drew our finest hairs
to fire
the deep, difficult troughs
unvoiced)
I fell through a basement railing
the first day of school and cut my forehead open—
did I ever tell you? More than forty years

and I still remember smelling my own blood
like the smell of a new schoolbook

And did you ever tell me
how your mother called you in from play
and from whom? To what? These atoms filmed by ordinary dust
that common life we each and all bent out of orbit from
to which we must return simply to say
this is where I came from
this is what I knew

The past is not a husk   yet change goes on

Freedom. It isn't once, to walk out
under the Milky Way, feeling the rivers
of light, the fields of dark—
freedom is daily, prose-bound, routine
remembering. Putting together, inch by inch
the starry worlds. From all the lost collections.

1979

WHAT IS POSSIBLE

A clear night   if the mind were clear

If the mind were simple, if the mind were bare
of all but the most classic necessities:
wooden spoon   knife   mirror
cup   lamp   chisel
a comb passing through hair beside a window
a sheet
          thrown back by the sleeper

A clear night in which two planets
seem to clasp each other   in which the earthly grasses
shift like silk in starlight
                    If the mind were clear
and if the mind were simple   you could take this mind
this particular state   and say
This is how I would live if I could choose:
this is what is possible

A clear night.   But the mind
of the woman imagining all this   the mind
that allows all this to be possible
is not clear as the night
is never simple   cannot clasp
its truths as the transiting planets clasp each other
does not so easily
                    work free from remorse
does not so easily
                    manage the miracle
for which mind is famous
                    or used to be famous

does not at will become abstract and pure

this woman's mind

does not even will that miracle
having a different mission
                              in the universe

If the mind were simple   if the mind were bare
it might resemble a room   a swept interior
but how could this now be possible

given the voices of the ghost-towns
their tiny and vast configurations
needing to be deciphered
                              the oracular night
with its densely working sounds

If it could ever come down to anything like
a comb passing through hair beside a window

no more than that
                    a sheet
                    thrown back by the sleeper
but the mind
of the woman thinking this   is wrapped in battle
is on another mission
a stalk of grass   dried feathery weed   rooted in snow
in frozen air stirring   a fierce wand graphing

Her finger also tracing
pages of a book

knowing better than the poem she reads
knowing through the poem

                            through ice-feathered panes
the winter

          flexing its talons
the hawk-wind

          poised to kill

1980

FOR ETHEL ROSENBERG

convicted, with her husband,
of "conspiracy to commit
espionage"; killed in the
electric chair June 19, 1953

I.
Europe 1953:
throughout my random sleepwalk
the words

scratched on walls, on pavements
painted over railway arches
Liberez les Rosenberg!

Escaping from home I found
home everywhere:
the Jewish question, Communism

marriage itself
a question of loyalty
or punishment

my Jewish father writing me
letters of seventeen pages
finely inscribed harangues

questions of loyalty
and punishment
One week before my wedding

that couple gets the chair
the volts grapple her, don't
kill her fast enough

Liberez les Rosenberg!
I hadn't realized
our family arguments were so important

my narrow understanding
of crime   of punishment
no language for this torment

mystery of that marriage
always both faces
on every front page in the world

Something so shocking   so
unfathomable
it must be pushed aside

2.
She sank however into my soul   A weight of sadness
I hardly can register how deep
her memory has sunk   that wife and mother

like so many
who seemed to get nothing out of any of it
except her children

that daughter   of a family
like so many
needing its female monster

she, actually wishing to be   *an artist*
wanting out of poverty
possibly also really wanting
                              revolution

that woman   strapped in the chair

no fear and no regrets
charged by posterity

not with selling secrets to the Communists
but with wanting   *to distinguish*
herself   being a bad daughter   a bad mother

And I   walking to my wedding
by the same token a bad daughter   a bad sister
my forces focussed

on that hardly revolutionary effort
Her life and death   the possible
ranges of disloyalty

so painful   so unfathomable
they must be pushed aside
ignored for years

3.
Her mother testifies against her
Her brother testifies against her
After her death

she becomes a natural prey for pornographers
her death itself a scene
her body *sizzling   half-strapped   whipped like a sail*

She becomes the extremest victim
described nonetheless as *rigid of will*
what are her politics by then   no one knows

Her figure sinks into my soul
a drowned statue
sealed in lead

For years it has lain there   unabsorbed
first as part of that dead couple
on the front pages of the world   the week

I gave myself in marriage
then slowly severing   drifting apart
a separate death   a life unto itself

no longer *the Rosenbergs*
no longer the chosen scapegoat
the family monster

till I hear how she sang
a prostitute to sleep
in the Women's House of Detention

Ethel Greenglass Rosenberg   would you
have marched to take back the night
collected signatures

for battered women who kill
What would you have to tell us
would you have burst the net

4.
Why do I even want to call her up
to console my pain   (she feels no pain at all)
why do I wish to put such questions

to ease myself   (she feels no pain at all
she   finally burned to death   like so many)
why all this exercise of hindsight?

since   if I imagine her at all
I have to imagine first
the pain inflicted on her   by women

her mother testifies against her
her sister-in-law testifies against her
and how she sees it

not the impersonal forces
not the historical reasons
why they might have hated her strength

If I have held her at arm's length till now
if I have still believed it was
my loyalty, my punishment at stake

if I dare imagine her surviving
I must be fair to what she must have lived through
I must allow her to be at last

political in her ways   not in mine
her urgencies perhaps   impervious to mine
defining revolution as she defines it

or, bored to the marrow of her bones
with "politics"
bored with the vast boredom of long pain

small; tiny in fact; in her late sixties
liking her room   her private life
living alone perhaps

no one you could interview
maybe filling a notebook herself
with secrets she has never sold

1980

MOTHER-IN-LAW

Tell me something
> you say
Not: What are you working on now, is there anyone special,
how is the job
do you mind coming back to an empty house
what do you do on Sundays
Tell me something . . .
> Some secret
we both know and have never spoken?
Some sentence that could flood with light
your life, mine?
Tell me what daughters tell their mothers
everywhere in the world, and I and only I
even have to ask. . . .
Tell me something.
> Lately, I hear it: Tell me something true,
> daughter-in-law, before we part,
> tell me something true before I die

And time was when I tried. *she accepts the daughter-in-law*
You married my son, and so only b/c the is the wife of her son.
strange as you are, you're my daughter
Tell me. . . .
> I've been trying to tell you, mother-in-law *role conflict in earlier life↑*
> that I think I'm breaking in two *mother-in-law was not*
> and half of me doesn't even want to love *there to help her*
> I can polish this table to satin because I don't care
> I am trying to tell you, I envy
> the people in mental hospitals their freedom
> and I can't live on placebos
> or Valium, like you

31

A cut lemon scours the smell of fish away
You'll feel better when the children are in school

I would try to tell you, mother-in-law
but my anger takes fire from yours and in the oven
the meal bursts into flames
Daughter-in-law, before we part
tell me something true

    I polished the table, mother-in-law
    and scrubbed the knives with half a lemon
    the way you showed me to do
    I wish I could tell you—

            Tell me!

They think I'm weak and hold
things back from me. I agreed to this years ago.
Daughter-in-law, strange as you are,
tell me something true

tell me something

        Your son is dead
    ten years, I am a lesbian,
    my children are themselves.
    Mother-in-law, before we part
    shall we try again? Strange as I am,
    strange as you are? What do mothers
    ask their own daughters, everywhere in the world?
    Is there a question?
            Ask me something.

1980

HEROINES

Exceptional
            even deviant
                        you draw your long skirts
across the nineteenth century
                        Your mind
burns long after death
                        not like the harbor beacon
but like a pyre of driftwood
                        on the beach
                                    You are spared
illiteracy
            death by pneumonia
                        teeth which leave the gums
the seamstress' clouded eyes
                        the mill-girl's shortening breath
by a collection
            of circumstances
                        soon to be known as
class privilege
            The law says you can possess nothing
                                    in a world
where property is everything
                        You belong first to your father
then to him who
            chooses you
                        if you fail to marry
you are without recourse
                        unable to earn
                                    a workingman's salary
forbidden to vote
            forbidden to speak
                        in public

if married you are legally dead

                              the law says

you may not bequeath property

                         save to your children

or male kin

          that your husband

                         has the right

of the slaveholder

                to hunt down and re-possess you

                                        should you escape

You may inherit slaves

                    but have no power to free them

your skin is fair

              you have been taught that light

came

     to the Dark Continent

                         with white power

that the Indians

             live in filth

                    and occult animal rites

Your mother wore corsets

                   to choke her spirit

                              which if you refuse

you are jeered for refusing

                     you have heard many sermons

and have carried

          your own interpretations

                         locked in your heart

You are a woman

              strong in health

                         through a collection

of circumstances

             soon to be known

                    as class privilege

which if you break

        the social compact

                you lose outright

When you open your mouth in public

              human excrement

                    is flung at you

you are exceptional

        in personal circumstance

              in indignation

you give up believing

        in protection

          in Scripture

in man-made laws

        respectable as you look

            you are an outlaw

Your mind burns

        not like the harbor beacon

           but like a fire

of fiercer origin

        you begin speaking out

and a great gust of freedom

        rushes in with your words

yet still you speak

        in the shattered language

           of a partial vision

You draw your long skirts

        deviant

          across the nineteenth century

registering injustice

        failing to make it whole

How can I fail to love

        your clarity and fury

how can I give you

        all your due

          take courage from your courage

35

honor your exact
                    legacy as it is
recognizing
            as well
                    that it is not enough?

1980

GRANDMOTHERS

1. Mary Gravely Jones

We had no petnames, no diminutives for you,
always the formal guest under my father's roof:
you were "Grandmother Jones" and you visited rarely.
I see you walking up and down the garden,
restless, southern-accented, reserved, you did not seem
my mother's mother or anyone's grandmother.
You were Mary, widow of William, and no matriarch,
yet smoldering to the end with frustrate life,
ideas nobody listened to, least of all my father.
One summer night you sat with my sister and me
in the wooden glider long after twilight,
holding us there with streams of pent-up words.
You could quote every poet I had ever heard of,
had read *The Opium Eater,* Amiel and Bernard Shaw,
your green eyes looked clenched against opposition.
You married straight out of the convent school,
your background was country, you left an unperformed
typescript of a play about Burr and Hamilton,
you were impotent and brilliant, no one cared
about your mind, you might have ended
elsewhere than in that glider
reciting your unwritten novels to the children.

2. Hattie Rice Rich

Your sweetness of soul was a mystery to me,
you who slip-covered chairs, glued broken china,
lived out of a wardrobe trunk in our guestroom
summer and fall, then took the Pullman train
in your darkblue dress and straw hat, to Alabama,
shuttling half-yearly between your son and daughter.
Your sweetness of soul was a convenience for everyone,
how you rose with the birds and children, boiled your own egg,
fished for hours on a pier, your umbrella spread,
took the street-car downtown shopping
endlessly for your son's whims, the whims of genius,
kept your accounts in ledgers, wrote letters daily.
All through World War Two the forbidden word
Jewish was barely uttered in your son's house;
your anger flared over inscrutable things.
Once I saw you crouched on the guestroom bed,
knuckles blue-white around the bedpost, sobbing
your one brief memorable scene of rebellion:
you didn't want to go back South that year.
You were never ''Grandmother Rich'' but ''Anana'';
you had money of your own but you were homeless,
Hattie, widow of Samuel, and no matriarch,
dispersed among the children and grandchildren.

3. Granddaughter

Easier to encapsulate your lives
in a slide-show of impressions given and taken,
to play the child or victim, the projectionist,
easier to invent a script for each of you,
myself still at the center,
than to write words in which you might have found
yourselves, looked up at me and said
"Yes, I was like that; but I was something more. . . ."
Danville, Virginia; Vicksburg, Mississippi;
the "war between the states" a living memory
its aftermath the plague-town closing
its gates, trying to cure itself with poisons.
I can almost touch that little town. . . .
a little white town rimmed with Negroes,
making a deep shadow on the whiteness.
Born a white woman, Jewish or of curious mind
—twice an outsider, still believing in inclusion—
in those defended hamlets of half-truth
broken in two by one strange idea,
"blood" the all-powerful, awful theme—
what were the lessons to be learned? If I believe
the daughter of one of you—Amnesia was the answer.

1980

THE SPIRIT OF PLACE

FOR MICHELLE CLIFF

I.

Over the hills in Shutesbury, Leverett
driving with you in spring   road
like a streambed unwinding downhill
fiddlehead ferns uncurling
spring peepers ringing sweet and cold

while we talk yet again
of dark and light, of blackness, whiteness, numbness
rammed through the heart like a stake
trying to pull apart the threads
from the dried blood of the old murderous uncaring

halting on bridges in bloodlight
where the freshets call out freedom
to frog-thrilling swamp, skunk-cabbage
trying to sense the conscience of these hills

knowing how the single-minded, pure
solutions bleached and dessicated
within their perfect flasks

for it was not enough to be New England
as every event since has testified:
New England's a shadow-country, always was

it was not enough to be for abolition
while the spirit of the masters
flickered in the abolitionist's heart

it was not enough to name ourselves anew
while the spirit of the masters
calls the freedwoman to forget the slave

With whom do you believe your lot is cast?
If there's a conscience in these hills
it hurls that question

unquenched, relentless, to our ears
wild and witchlike
ringing every swamp

II.
The mountain laurel in bloom
constructed like needlework
tiny half-pulled stitches piercing
flushed and stippled petals

here in these woods it grows wild
midsummer moonrise turns it opal
the night breathes with its clusters
protected species

meaning endangered
Here in these hills
this valley   we have felt
a kind of freedom

planting the soil   have known
hours of a calm, intense and mutual solitude
reading and writing
trying to clarify   connect

past and present   near and far
the Alabama quilt
the Botswana basket
history   the dark crumble

of last year's compost
filtering softly through your living hand

but here as well we face
instantaneous violence   ambush   male

dominion on a back road
to escape in a locked car   windows shut
skimming the ditch   your split-second
survival reflex taking on the world

as it is   not as we wish it
as it is   not as we work for it
to be

III.
Strangers are an endangered species

In Emily Dickinson's house in Amherst
cocktails are served   the scholars
gather in celebration
their pious or clinical legends
festoon the walls like imitations
of period patterns

    (. . . *and, as I feared, my "life" was made a "victim"*)

The remnants pawed   the relics
the cult assembled in the bedroom

and you   whose teeth were set on edge by churches
resist your shrine
             escape
                are found
nowhere
        unless in words   (your own)

All we are strangers—dear—The world is not
acquainted with us, because we are not acquainted
with her. And Pilgrims!—Do you hesitate? and
Soldiers oft—some of us victors, but those I do
not see tonight owing to the smoke.—We are hungry,
and thirsty, sometimes—We are barefoot—and cold—

This place is large enough for both of us
the river-fog will do for privacy
this is my third and last address to you

with the hands of a daughter I would cover you
from all intrusion   even my own
saying   rest to your ghost

with the hands of a sister I would leave your hands
open or closed as they prefer to lie
and ask no more of who or why or wherefore

with the hands of a mother I would close the door
on the rooms you've left behind
and silently pick up my fallen work

IV.
The river-fog will do for privacy
on the low road a breath
here, there, a cloudiness floating on the blacktop

sunflower heads turned black and bowed
the seas of corn a stubble
the old routes flowing north, if not to freedom

no human figure now in sight
(with whom do you believe your lot is cast?)
only the functional figure of the scarecrow

the cut corn, ground to shreds, heaped in a shape
like an Indian burial mound
a haunted-looking, ordinary thing

The work of winter starts fermenting in my head
how with the hands of a lover or a midwife
to hold back till the time is right

force nothing, be unforced
accept no giant miracles of growth
by counterfeit light

trust roots, allow the days to shrink
give credence to these slender means
wait without sadness and with grave impatience

here in the north where winter has a meaning
where the heaped colors suddenly go ashen
where nothing is promised

learn what an underground journey
has been, might have to be; speak in a winter code
let fog, sleet, translate; wind, carry them.

V.
Orion plunges like a drunken hunter
over the Mohawk Trail   a parallelogram
slashed with two cuts of steel

A night so clear that every constellation
stands out from an undifferentiated cloud
of stars, a kind of aura

All the figures up there look violent to me
as a pogrom on Christmas Eve in some old country
I want our own earth   not the satellites, our

world as it is   if not as it might be
then as it is: male dominion, gangrape, lynching, pogrom
the Mohawk wraiths in their tracts of leafless birch

watching: will we do better?
The tests I need to pass are prescribed by the spirits
of place   who understand travel but not amnesia

The world as it is: not as her users boast
damaged beyond reclamation by their using
Ourselves as we are   in these painful motions

of staying cognizant: some part of us always
out beyond ourselves
knowing   knowing   knowing

Are we all in training for something we don't name?
to exact reparation for things
done long ago to us and to those who did not

survive what was done to them   whom we ought to honor
with grief   with fury   with action
On a pure night   on a night when pollution

seems absurdity when the undamaged planet seems to turn
like a bowl of crystal in black ether
they are the piece of us that lies out there
knowing   knowing   knowing

1980

FRAME

Winter twilight. She comes out of the lab-
oratory, last class of the day
a pile of notebooks slung in her knapsack, coat
zipped high against the already swirling
evening sleet. The wind is wicked and the
busses slower than usual. On her mind
is organic chemistry and the issue
of next month's rent and will it be possible to
bypass the professor with the coldest eyes
to get a reference for graduate school,
and whether any of them, even those who smile
can see, looking at her, a biochemist
or a marine biologist, which of the faces
can she trust to see her at all, either today
or in any future. The busses are worm-slow in the
quickly gathering dark. *I don't know her. I am
standing though somewhere just outside the frame
of all this, trying to see.* At her back
the newly finished building suddenly looks
like shelter, it has glass doors, lighted halls
presumably heat. The wind is wicked. She throws a
glance down the street, sees no bus coming and runs
up the newly constructed steps into the newly
constructed hallway. *I am standing all this time
just beyond the frame, trying to see.* She runs
her hand through the crystals of sleet about to melt
on her hair. She shifts the weight of the books
on her back. It isn't warm here exactly but it's
out of that wind. Through the glass
door panels she can watch for the bus through the thickening
weather. Watching so, she is not
watching for the white man who watches the building

46

who has been watching her. This is Boston 1979.
I am standing somewhere at the edge of the frame
watching the man, we are both white, who watches the building
telling her to move on, get out of the hallway.
I can hear nothing because I am not supposed to be
present but I can see her gesturing
out toward the street at the wind-raked curb
I see her drawing her small body up
against the implied charges. The man
goes away. Her body is different now.
It is holding together with more than a hint of fury
and more than a hint of fear. She is smaller, thinner
more fragile-looking than I am. *But I am not supposed to be*
there. I am just outside the frame
of this action when the anonymous white man
returns with a white police officer. Then she starts
to leave into the windraked night but already
the policeman is going to work, the handcuffs are on her
wrists he is throwing her down his knee has gone into
her breast he is dragging her down the stairs *I am unable*
to hear a sound of all this all that I know is what
I can see from this position there is no soundtrack
to go with this and I understand at once
it is meant to be in silence that this happens
in silence that he pushes her into the car
banging her head in silence that she cries out
in silence that she tries to explain she was only
waiting for a bus
in silence that he twists the flesh of her thigh
with his nails in silence that her tears begin to flow
that she pleads with the other policeman as if
he could be trusted to see her at all
in silence that in the precinct she refuses to give her name
in silence that they throw her into the cell
in silence that she stares him

noone wants to see or hear this but it is real

47

straight in the face in silence that he sprays her
in her eyes with Mace in silence that she sinks her teeth
into his hand in silence that she is charged
with trespass assault and battery in
silence that at the sleet-swept corner her bus
passes without stopping and goes on
in silence. *What I am telling you*
is told by a white woman who they will say
was never there. I say I am there.

1980

RIFT

I have in my head some images of you:
your face turned awkwardly from the kiss of greeting
the sparkle of your eyes in the dark car, driving
your beautiful fingers reaching for
a glass of water.
            Also your lip curling
at what displeases you, the sign of closure,
the fending-off, the clouding-over.
                      Politics,
you'd say, *is an unworthy name
for what we're after.*
            What we're after
is not that clear to me, if politics
is an unworthy name.

When language fails us, when we fail each other
there is no exorcism. The hurt continues. Yes, your scorn
turns up the jet of my anger. Yes, I find you
overweening, obsessed, and even in your genius
narrow-minded—I could list much more—
and absolute loyalty was never in my line
once having left it in my father's house—
but as I go on sorting images of you
my hand trembles, and I try
to train it not to tremble.

1980

49

A VISION

(*thinking of Simone Weil*)

You. There, with your gazing eyes
Your blazing eyes

A hand or something passes across the sun. Your eyeballs slacken,
you are free for a moment. Then it comes back: this
test of the capacity to keep in focus
this
     unfair struggle with the forces of perception
this enforced
               (but at that word your attention changes)
this enforced   loss of self
in a greater thing of course, who has ever
lost herself in something smaller?

You with your cornea and iris and their power
you with your stubborn lids that have stayed open
at the moment of pouring liquid steel
you with your fear of blinding

Here it is. I am writing this almost
involuntarily on a bad, a junky typewriter that skips
and slides the text
Still these are mechanical problems, writing to you
is another kind of problem
and even so the words create themselves

What is your own will that it
can so transfix you
why are you forced to take this test
over and over and call it God
why not call it you and get it over

50

you with your hatred of enforcement
and your fear of blinding?

1981

TURNING THE WHEEL

1. Location

No room for nostalgia here. What would it look like?
The imitation of a ghost mining town,
the movie-set façade of a false Spanish
arcade, the faceless pueblo
with the usual faceless old woman grinding corn?
It's all been done. Acre on acre
of film locations disguised as Sears,
Safeway, the Desert National Bank,
Fashion Mall, Sun Valley Waterbeds.
Old people, rich, pass on in cloistered stucco
tiled and with fountains; poor, at Golden Acres
Trailer Ranch for Adult Seniors, at the edge of town,
close by the Reassembled Church of Latter-Day
Saints and a dozen motels called Mountain View.
The mountains are on view from everywhere
in this desert: this poor, conquered, bulldozed desert
overridden like a hold-out
enemy village. Nostalgia for the desert
will soon draw you to the Desert Museum
or off on an unpaved track to stare at one saguaro
—velvety, pleated, from a distance graceful—
closer-on, shot through with bullet holes
and seeming to give the finger to it all.

2. Burden Baskets

False history gets made all day, any day,
the truth of the new is never on the news
False history gets written every day
and by some who should know better:
the lesbian archaeologist watches herself
sifting her own life out from the shards she's piecing,
asking the clay all questions but her own.
Yet suddenly for once the standard version
splits open to something shocking, unintentional.
In the elegant Southwest Museum, no trace of bloodshed
or broken treaty. But, behind glass, these baskets
woven for the young women's puberty dances
still performed among the still surviving
Apache people;   filled with offerings:
cans of diet Pepsi, peanut brittle,
Cracker Jack, Hershey bars
piled there, behind glass, without notation
in the anthropologist's typewritten text
which like a patient voice tired of explaining
goes on to explain a different method of weaving.

3. Hohokam

Nostalgia is only amnesia turned around.
I try to pierce through to a prehistoric culture
the museum says were known as *those who have ceased*.
I try to imagine them, before the Hopi
or Navaho, *those who have ceased*
but they draw back, an archetypal blur.
Did they leave behind for Pima or Navaho
something most precious, now archaic,
more than a faceless woman grinding corn?
Those who have ceased is amnesia-language:
no more to be said of them. Nobody wants
to see their faces or hear what they were about.
I try to imagine a desert-shamaness
bringing water to fields of squash, maize and cotton
but where the desert herself is half-eroded
half-flooded by a million jets of spray
to conjure a rich white man's paradise
the shamaness could well have withdrawn her ghost.

4. Self-hatred

In Colcha embroidery, I learn,
women use ravelled yarn from old wool blankets
to trace out scenes on homespun woollen sacks—
our ancient art of making out of nothing—
or is it making the old life serve the new?
The impact of Christian culture, it is written,
and other influences, have changed the patterns.
(*Once they were birds perhaps,* I think; *or serpents.*)
Example: here we have a scene of flagellants,
each whip is accurately self-directed.
To understand colonization is taking me
years. I stuck my loaded needle
into the coarse squares of the sack, I smoothed
the stylized pattern on my knee with pride.
I also heard them say my own designs
were childlike, primitive, obscene.
What rivets me to history is seeing
arts of survival turned
to rituals of self-hatred. This
is colonization. Unborn sisters,
look back on us in mercy where we failed ourselves,
see us not one-dimensional but with
the past as your steadying and corrective lens.

5. Particularity

In search of the desert witch, the shamaness
forget the archetypes, forget the dark
and lithic profile, do not scan the clouds
massed on the horizon, violet and green,
for her icon, do not pursue
the ready-made abstraction, do not peer for symbols.
So long as you want her faceless, without smell
or voice, so long as she does not squat
to urinate, or scratch herself, so long
as she does not snore beneath her blanket
or grimace as she grasps the stone-cold
grinding stone at dawn
so long as she does not have her own peculiar
face, slightly wall-eyed or with a streak
of topaz lightning in the blackness
of one eye, so long as she does not limp
so long as you try to simplify her meaning
so long as she merely symbolizes power
she is kept helpless and conventional
her true power routed backward
into the past, we cannot touch or name her
and, barred from participation by those who need her
she stifles in unspeakable loneliness.

6. Apparition

If she appears, hands ringed with rings
you have dreamed about, if on her large fingers
jasper and sardonyx and agate smolder
if she is wearing shawls woven in fire
and blood, if she is wearing shawls
of undyed fiber, yellowish
if on her neck are hung
obsidian and silver, silver and turquoise
if she comes skirted like a Christian
her hair combed back by missionary fingers
if she sits offering her treasure by the road
to spare a brother's or an uncle's dignity
or if she sits pretending
to weave or grind or do some other thing
for the appeasement of the ignorant
if she is the famous potter
whose name confers honor on certain vessels
if she is wrist-deep in mud and shawled in dust
and wholly anonymous
look at her closely if you dare
do not assume you know those cheekbones
or those eye-sockets; or that still-bristling hair.

7. Mary Jane Colter, 1904

My dear Mother and Sister:
                                    I have been asked
to design a building in the Hopi style
at the Grand Canyon. As you know
in all my travels for Mr. Harvey
and the Santa Fe Railroad, I have thought this the greatest
sight in the Southwest—in our land entire.
I am here already, trying to make a start.
I cannot tell you with what elation
this commission has filled me. I regret to say
it will mean I cannot come home to St. Paul
as I hoped, this spring. I am hoping this may lead
to other projects here, of equal grandeur.
(Do you understand? I want this glory,
I want to place my own conception
and that of the Indians whose land this was
at the edge of this incommensurable thing.)
I know my life seems shaky, unreliable
to you. When this is finished I promise you
to come home to St. Paul and teach. You will never lack
for what I can give you. Your affectionate
daughter and sister,
                        Mary.

8. Turning the Wheel

The road to the great canyon always feels
like that road and no other
the highway to a fissure   to the female core
of a continent
Below Flagstaff even   the rock erosions wear
a famous handwriting
the river's still prevailing signature

Seeing those rocks   that road   in dreams   I know
it is happening again   as twice while waking
I am travelling to the edge   to meet the face
of annihilating and impersonal time
stained in the colors of a woman's genitals
outlasting every transient violation
a face that is strangely intimate to me

Today I turned the wheel   refused that journey
I was feeling too alone on the open plateau
of piñon juniper   world beyond time
of rockflank spread around me   too alone
and too filled with you   with whom I talked for hours
driving up from the desert   though you were far away
as I talk to you all day   whatever day

1981

"The Images": The phrase "moral and ordinary" is echoed from Blanche Wiesen Cook's essay "Female Support Networks and Political Activism" in her pamphlet *Women and Support Networks* (Brooklyn: Out & Out Books, 1979).

"Integrity": To my knowledge, this word was first introduced in a feminist context by Janice Raymond in her essay "The Illusion of Androgyny," *Quest: A Feminist Quarterly* 2, no. 1 (Summer 1975).

"Culture and Anarchy": The title is stolen from Matthew Arnold's collection of essays by the same name, first published in London, 1869. The sources for the voices of nineteenth-century women heard in this poem are as follows: Diaries of Susan B. Anthony, 1861; letter from Anthony to her sister, 1883, both from Ida Husted Harper, *The Life and Work of Susan B. Anthony* (Indianapolis and Kansas City: Bowen-Merrill, 1899); Jane Addams, *Twenty Years at Hull House* (New York: Macmillan, 1926); Elizabeth Barrett-Browning, letter to Anna Brownell Jameson, 1852, in Frederick Kenyon, ed., *The Letters of Elizabeth Barrett Browning* (New York: Macmillan, 1898), vol. 2; Ida Husted Harper, introduction to Susan B. Anthony and Ida Husted Harper, *The History of Woman Suffrage* (1902) vol. 4; Elizabeth Cady Stanton, speech "On Solitude of Self," in Anthony and Harper, *The History of Woman Suffrage,* vol. 4; Elizabeth Cady Stanton, letter to Susan B. Anthony, in Harper, *The Life and Work of Susan B. Anthony,* vol. i.

"For Julia in Nebraska": Epigraph quoted from the Willa Cather Educational Foundation, Historical Landmark Council, marker at the intersection of Highways 281 and 4, fourteen miles north of Red Cloud, Nebraska.

"For Ethel Rosenberg": Phrases italicized in section 3, line 6, are from Robert Coover's novel, *The Public Burning of Julius and Ethel Rosenberg* (New York: Viking, 1977).

"Mother-in-Law": It has been suggested to me that the lines "I am trying to tell you, I envy/the people in mental hospitals their freedom" add to a stockpile of false images of mental patients' incarceration—

images which help perpetuate their pain and the system which routinely drugs, curbs, "constrains," electroshocks, and surgically experiments on them. The woman speaking in the poem speaks, of course, out of her own frustration and despair, the lines are bitterly ironic; but I agree with my critics that in a world eager both to romanticize and to torture mental patients, such clichés must be used, if at all, with utmost concern for the realities underlying them.

"Heroines": See Gerda Lerner: "The history of notable women is the history of exceptional, even deviant women, and does not describe the experience and history of the mass of women" ("Placing Women in History: Definitions and Challenges," in Gerda Lerner, *The Majority Finds Its Past* [New York: Oxford University Press, 1979]).

"Grandmothers: 3": Italicized lines are quoted from Lillian Smith's *Killers of the Dream* (New York: Norton, 1961), p. 39.

"The Spirit of Place: III": Italicized passages are from Thomas Johnson and Theodora Ward, eds., *The Letters of Emily Dickinson* (Cambridge, Mass.: Harvard University Press, 1958), specifically, from Letter 154 to Susan Gilbert (June 1854) and Letter 203 to Catherine Scott Anthon Turner (March 1859).

"Turning the Wheel: 3": The Hohokam were a prehistoric farming culture who developed irrigation canals in southern Arizona and southwestern New Mexico between about 300 B.C. and A.D. 1400. The word *Hohokam* is Pima and is translated variously as "those who have ceased" or "those who were used up." See Emil W. Haury, *The Hohokam, Desert Farmers and Craftsmen* (sic) (Tucson: University of Arizona Press, 1976).

"Turning the Wheel: 7": The letter is a poetic fiction, based on a reading of Virginia Grattan, *Mary Colter, Builder upon the Red Earth* (Flagstaff, Ariz.: Northland Press, 1980). Mary E. J. Colter (1869–1958) studied design and architecture in order to support her mother and younger sister upon her father's death. She taught art in a St. Paul, Minnesota, high school for fifteen years before starting to work as a decorator for the Fred Harvey Company and the Santa Fe Railroad. Soon she was completely in charge of both exterior and interior design of hotels and restaurants from Chicago westward. Her work advanced the movement away from Victorian style toward a more indigenous southwestern and western architecture. At the height of her career she designed eight major buildings at the

Grand Canyon, all of which are still standing. She never married. She drew consistently on Native American arts and design in her work, and her collection of Hopi and Navaho art can be seen at Mesa Verde Museum. Colter's lifework—a remarkable accomplishment for a woman architect—was thus inextricable from the violation and expropriation of Native culture by white entrepreneurs. Yet her love for that culture was lifelong.